KT-294-740

Bromley

Celebrate!

# Japan

Robyn Hardyman

W
FRANKLIN WATTS
LONDON•SYDNEY

This edition first published in 2009
by Franklin Watts



Franklin Watts
338 Euston Road
London NW1 3BH

Franklin Watts Australia
Level 17/207 Kent Street
Sydney, NSW 2000



A CIP catalogue record for this book is available from the British Library.
Dewey no: 915.2

ISBN 978 0 7496 8425 9

Printed in China

Franklin Watts is a division of Hachette Children's Books, an Hachette UK company.
www.hachette.co.uk

Note to parents and teachers concerning websites:
In the book every effort has been made by the Publishers to ensure that websites are suitable for children, that they are of the highest educational value, and that they contain no inappropriate or offensive material. However, because of the nature of the Internet, it is impossible to guarantee that the contents of these sites will not be altered. We advise that Internet access is supervised by a responsible adult.

**For The Brown Reference Group Ltd**
Project Editor: Sarah Eason
Designer: Paul Myerscough
Picture Researcher: Maria Joannou
Indexer: Claire Throp
Design Manager: David Poole
Managing Editor: Miranda Smith
Editorial Director: Lindsey Lowe

**Consultant Editor**
Peter Lewis
Writer and Editor for the American Geographical Society, New York

**Author**
Robyn Hardyman

**Picture Credits**
Front Cover: Shutterstock: Jose Gil, Hiroshi Ichikawa (t), Bata Ziranovic (b).

Alamy Images: The London Art Archive 21, BG Motorsports 11l, Chris Willson 19l; Corbis: Bass Museum of Art 20b, Manuel Blondeau/Photo & Co 12-13, Tibor Bognár 20t, R. Creation/amanaimages 28, Sakamoto Photo Research Laboratory 6t, 8t, Tokyo Space Club 16bl, ZONO/Amanaimages 18; Dreamstime: Batoots 10c, Zhang Lei 23t; Fotolia: Tororo Reaction 27br; Istockphoto: Sean Barley 26b, Frank Sebastian Hansen 29c, Troy Kennedy 26t, Tatiana Mironenko 16t, Jeremy Wee 14b; Library of Congress/US Navy 8b; Photolibrary: Japan Travel Bureau 5l, 7t; Rex Features: Roy Garner 15b, Olycom Spa 22t; Shutterstock: 9t, Gualtiero Boffi 14t, Phil Date 9bl, Sam Dcruz 3t, 4, eAlisa 17t, EveStock 19r, Ilya D. Gridnev 29b, Jaroslaw Grudzinski 16br, Hiroshi Ichikawa 5r, Katariina Järvinen 25tr, kentoh 17b, Steve Luker 27bl, Martin Mette 6b, 9br, 22bl, Phillip Minnis 23b, Walter Pall 27t, Raimik 27c, Jose Antonio Sanchez 15t, Tristan Scholze 29t, Elena Schweitzer 22br, Kiselev Andrey Valerevich 3b; Wikipedia: 13b, Sakurambo 12b.

# Contents

# Welcome to Japan

*Japan is a country in East Asia. It is made up of a collection of islands in the Pacific Ocean. Japan is a beautiful country with a fascinating history. Today, it is one of the top manufacturing nations in the world and has become a very wealthy country.*

Japan is highly mountainous, and much of the land is unsuitable for agriculture, industry or even **residential** use. Most of the people live in flatter coastal areas.

## Tokyo

Tokyo is Japan's capital city. It is on the eastern side of the main island, Honshu, and is home to the Japanese government, the *emperor* and the Imperial Palace. Modern Tokyo is a bustling and crowded place, with a population of more than twelve million people!

## Japan's islands

Japan has more than 3,000 islands, but most people live on the four biggest: Honshu, Hokkaido, Shikoku and Kyushu. Honshu is the largest island, and is often called the mainland. Russia, Korea and China are about 480 km to the west of Japan. The United States and Canada are to the east, about 7,000 km across the Pacific Ocean.

## JAPANESE FACTS

| | |
|---|---|
| FULL NAME | *Japan* |
| CAPITAL CITY | *Tokyo* |
| AREA | *377,835 square km* |
| POPULATION IN 2007 | *128 million* |
| MAIN LANGUAGES | *Japanese* |
| MAIN RELIGIONS | *Shintoism, Buddhism* |
| CURRENCY | *Yen* |

## *Longest bridge*

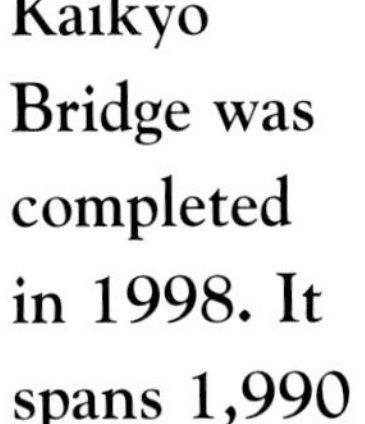

**The Akashi Kaikyo Bridge was completed in 1998. It spans 1,990 metres, and is the world's longest** suspension bridge**. It links Kobe on Honshu to the island of Awaji.**

## Mount Fuji

**The peak of Mount Fuji is one of Japan's most famous landmarks and is a sacred, or holy, place for the Japanese people. In summer, thousands of** pilgrims **climb to the top of the mountain to watch the beautiful sunrise.**

**WEB LINKS**

**To find out more about Mount Fuji, go to:**
**http://www.jnto.go.jp/eng/location/regional/shizuoka/fujisan.html**

# History Highlights

*By 400 C.E. Japan was a united country, with an emperor as its head of state. For centuries, it resisted invasion and remained cut off from the outside world. This helped it develop its own fascinating society and way of life.*

During the Jomon period (13000–300 B.C.E.), Japan was **inhabited** by **nomadic** hunters and gatherers, who left behind some of the world's oldest pottery. As farming developed, people began to settle into groups, ruled by large landowners. Around 300 C.E., the head of the Yamato group became the most powerful chief. Over the next 250 years, Yamato leaders united the groups into one nation under one leader.

## Capital cities

In 710 C.E., Empress Gemmei founded a new capital city at Nara, and many Buddhist temples were built there. In 794 C.E., Emperor Kammu moved the capital to Kyoto, because the Buddhist priests at Nara were becoming too powerful. Kyoto remained the capital city until 1868.

## *Shoguns and samurai*

The emperor was not the most powerful figure in Japan. Real power lay with the noble families, or daimyo, who owned much of the land. In the 1160s, war broke out between two of these families, the Minamoto and the Taira. The Minamoto won. The emperor gave the leader of the family, Minamoto Yoritomo, the title of shogun. This means 'supreme general'. The rule of the shoguns lasted for 700 years. During this time, rival daimyo chiefs fought each other for the title. They were supported by armies of samurai warriors (below). These ferocious fighters lived by a strict code of discipline.

## Edo period

During the fourteenth and sixteenth centuries, there were bloody wars between rival daimyo. Peace finally arrived with shogun Tokugawa Ieyasu, who was based in Edo (now Tokyo). The daimyo ruled their local areas, but were also loyal to the shogun. The cities grew in the peaceful Edo period and people became richer. The arts blossomed, and beautiful paintings were created during this time (above). However, there was little contact with the West because the Tokugawa were afraid of invasion. Laws forbade people to leave Japan, and Western books were banned.

DID YOU KNOW?
The Japanese have the longest reigning dynasty in the world. The present emperor – Emperor Akihito – is 125th in a long line of rulers going back over 2,000 years.

## Tokugawa Ieyasu (1543–1616)

**Shogun Tokugawa Ieyasu (left) was determined to control all of Japan. His military base was at a village called Edo. He transformed it into a large, successful city, with roads, canals and a castle. He set up a strict** social structure, **with four levels: samurai, farmers, craftsmen and merchants. Rules controlled where each group could live. The Tokugawa family ruled Japan peacefully for more than 250 years.**

## Building an empire

In the mid-nineteenth century, trade with the West was finally allowed. The daimyo chiefs overthrew the shogun, and the emperor began to rule Japan once more. Between 1868 and 1912, Japan developed into a modern industrial country. The samurai warrior class was **abolished**, and replaced with a modern army and navy. Railways and factories were built. Japan also began to build an empire in the Far East, taking different territories from Korea, Russia and China. In World War I (1914–18), Japan fought against Germany, and afterwards it continued to fight, and take territory from, China.

## *Pearl Harbor*

**In 1941, Japan attacked the American naval base at Pearl Harbor, Hawaii (below). Japan destroyed many warships. The act brought the United States into World War II.**

## Rising from the ashes

In 1945, Japan surrendered when **atomic bombs** were dropped on two of its cities, Nagasaki and Hiroshima. Japan recovered from the war quickly. In 1947, a new **constitution** changed the status of the emperor to a purely **ceremonial role**. He is still head of state, but he does not rule. Japan then grew to become a leading industrial nation. Japan's new industries made goods, such as cars, that were needed all over the world. The workers were well trained and skilful. In just four years between 1960 and 1964, Japan's average income doubled.

### World power

Today, Japan has the second largest economy in the world after the United States. Its computers, cars, televisions and music systems are sold everywhere. Japan is the world's largest car manufacturer. The two biggest makers of video games consoles, Sony and Nintendo, are both Japanese companies.

### *Country of contrasts*

**In modern Japanese cities, the old and the new live side by side. In Osaka, the old castle (shown above) is surrounded by modern offices.**

# Fly the Flag

*The national flag of Japan is white with a large red circle in the centre. The white represents purity and honesty, and the red circle represents the rising sun. The flag is best known as the Hinomaru, which means 'sun disc'. Japan is often called the 'Land of the Rising Sun'.*

The current Japanese **emblem** has been used on the national flag since 1870. It can be seen on the flags opposite. Japanese people are waving the flags to greet Emperor Akihito at the Imperial Palace on his birthday.

### Imperial flag

This is the flag of the Japanese emperor. It shows a gold chrysanthemum with sixteen petals on a red background. It has been in use since 1889.

## *Rising sun flag*

**A flag showing a sun disc with sixteen rays (below) has been used by warriors throughout Japan's history. The flag was first used by the Japanese Navy in 1889, and the Navy continued to use it until the end of World War II. This striking flag is still used today by the Japan Marine Self-defence Force.**

## Prefectures

Japan is divided into forty-seven areas called **prefectures**. Each one has its own flag. This is the flag of the prefecture of Saga, in western Kyushu.

 *Try this!*

## *Make a Japanese flag*

- *Take a sheet of white card and draw a rectangle that is exactly 18.75 cm long and 12.5 cm high. Cut out the rectangle.*
- *Using a ruler and pencil, draw a diagonal line from the top left corner of the rectangle to the bottom right corner. Now do the same from the top right corner to the bottom left corner. The point at which the lines meet in the middle is the centre of your circle.*
- *Using a pair of compasses, put the point on the centre mark and draw a circle that is 7.5 cm in diameter.*
- *Rub out your pencil marks and colour in the circle using red paint or felt-tip pen.*
- *Use sticky tape to attach your flag to a pencil or a thin stick. You have made a Japanese flag!*

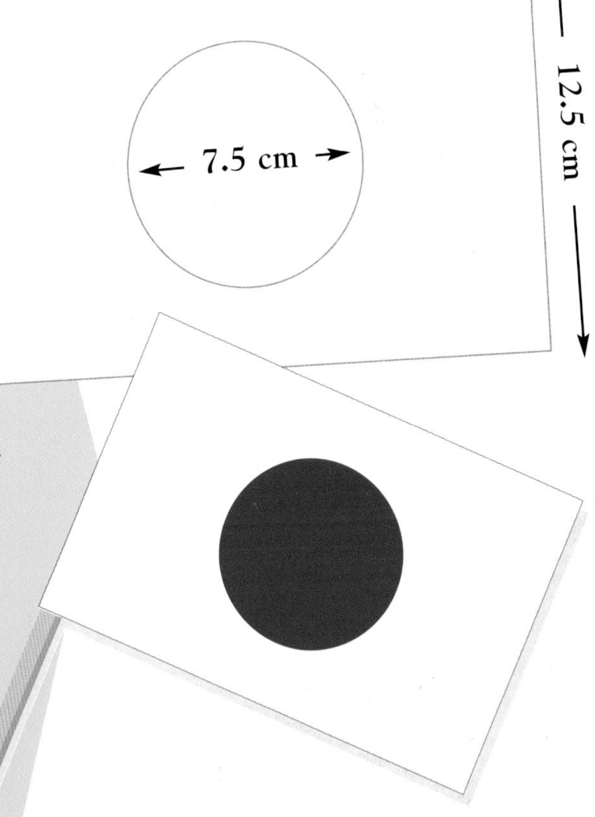

# Hymn to Japan

***Japan's national anthem is called* Kimi Ga Yo*, which means 'Our Emperor's Reign'. It is one of the shortest national anthems in the world.***

The words of the national anthem are taken from a poem that is about 1,000 years old. The poet himself is unknown. The words were set to music in 1880, to celebrate the birthday of the Emperor Meiji. The composer was Hiromori Hayashi, a musician at the Imperial Court. The song was then used as the national anthem in 1888. Below is the score of *Kimigayo* with its words in Japanese **characters**.

## The Japanese anthem in translation

Ten thousand years of
happy reign be yours.
Rule on, my lord, till what
are pebbles now
By ages united to mighty
rocks shall grow,
On whose venerable sides
the moss does grow.

## Team spirit

This picture shows the Japanese rugby players listening to their national anthem before playing an international game. On the left is their country's national flag.

## *National unity*

This is a *sazareishi* (right), a type of boulder that is made up of many pebbles. It is the symbol of unity mentioned within the Japanese national anthem. This stone stands in the grounds of Shimogamo Shrine in Kyoto.

WEB LINKS

To hear the Japanese national anthem go to: http://www.national-anthems.net/JA

DID YOU KNOW?

Although *Kimigayo* is one of the world's oldest national anthems, it was not officially recognized until 1999.

# Regions of Japan

*Japan stretches about 2,400 km from north to south. It is divided into eight regions, and these regions are divided into areas called prefectures. There is a great variety of landscape, climate and other geographical features across these regions.*

Most of inland Japan is mountainous. The cities, towns and farmland are squeezed on to the narrow **plains** around the coasts. Farmers grow rice, wheat, soya beans, tea, fruit and vegetables. On hillsides, rice is grown on narrow strips of land. Farmers also keep pigs and chickens. Fishing is a very important industry in Japan, and people eat a lot of fish.

## JAPANESE FACTS

| | |
|---|---|
| LONGEST RIVER | *Shinano 367 km* |
| HIGHEST MOUNTAIN | *Mount Fuji 3,776 m* |
| LARGEST CITIES | *Tokyo, Yokohama, Osaka, Nagoya, Sapporo* |
| NATIONAL PARKS | *Daisetsuzan, Hokkaidō; Kirishima-Yaku, Kyushū* |

## Climate

Japan has a varied climate. In its far north, winters are long, cold and often snowy. Summers in the north are short and cool. Central Japan has cool winters and warm summers. In the far south, summers are very hot and sticky. Monsoon winds bring heavy rain and snow.

## Rice fields

Only a small part of Japan can be used for farming, but the Japanese grow plenty of rice on narrow strips, called **terraces**.

## *Earthquakes and volcanoes*

**Japan suffers from about 1,500 earthquakes a year. Most are slight, but sometimes a huge earthquake causes devastation. Japan also has more than seventy active volcanoes. A severe earthquake hit the city of Kobe (below) in Honshu in 1995.**

## City and country

Most Japanese people work in crowded towns and cities. They live in large blocks of flats or small houses. In the countryside, the low-rise houses are made of wood. The *shinkansen*, or 'bullet trains', (above) travel at up to 300 km/h between cities. Honshu and Hokkaido are connected by the world's longest train tunnel, which is almost fifty-six kilometres long.

## *Typhoons*

**Tropical storms called** typhoons **strike Japan in autumn. They bring winds of more than 160 km/h, and rains that cause floods.**

WEB LINKS

**Find out more about Japan's wonderful National Parks at:**
**http://www.env.go.jp/en/nature/nps/park/**

# What's Cooking?

***Japanese people take a lot of care in choosing and preparing their food. Their diet is generally very healthy, with little meat, dairy or fat. This type of diet helps the Japanese to live longer than almost any other people in the world.***

Rice is the most important food in Japan. It is eaten at every meal – the Japanese word for rice also means 'a meal'. The Japanese version of fast food is noodles. Soba noodles are made from buckwheat flour, and udon noodles are made from white flour. They are often served in a hot soup, with pieces of meat, fish, egg or vegetables. Noodle bars are always busy at lunchtime.

**DID YOU KNOW?**
**The Japanese make a strong wine called *sake* from rice. It is drunk either hot or cold.**

## Eating customs

Japanese people generally eat sitting on cushions on the floor, around a low table. They eat with chopsticks. They always take their shoes off inside the house.

## Fish

Japanese people love fish. *Sashimi* is thin strips of raw fish, served with soy sauce and horseradish. *Sushi* is small patties of rice with vinegar, topped with raw fish, seaweed or vegetables. *Tempura* is a dish of deep-fried battered fish or vegetables.

## Tea

**Green tea is the most popular drink in Japan. It is drunk from a small china cup at mealtimes.**

## What's on the menu?

This family meal consists of three dishes that would be served at the same time.

**ramen**
soup with thin noodles, spring onions, egg and vegetables

**spinach gomaae**
side dish with sesame dressing

**gyudon**
sweet and salty dish of beef and onion served on cooked rice

## *Try this!*

### *Let's make Yakitori*

***Ingredients:***

*60 ml soy sauce*
*45 ml sugar*
*15 ml honey or maple syrup*
*3 chicken thighs, boned and skinned*
*6 small wooden skewers*
*1 leek*

*Ask an adult to help you with the chopping and cooking. Mix the soy sauce, sugar and honey or maple syrup with a little warm water. Cut the chicken into 2.5 cm pieces. Put them in the sauce and leave for an hour. Soak the wooden skewers in warm water. Cut the leek into pieces about 5 cm long. Spear three or four pieces of chicken and some leek on to each wooden skewer. Cook the yakitori under a hot grill for about 5–10 minutes, or in an oven at 200°C for about 15 minutes.*

# How Do I Say...?

***Japanese is a complicated language that takes many years to learn.***

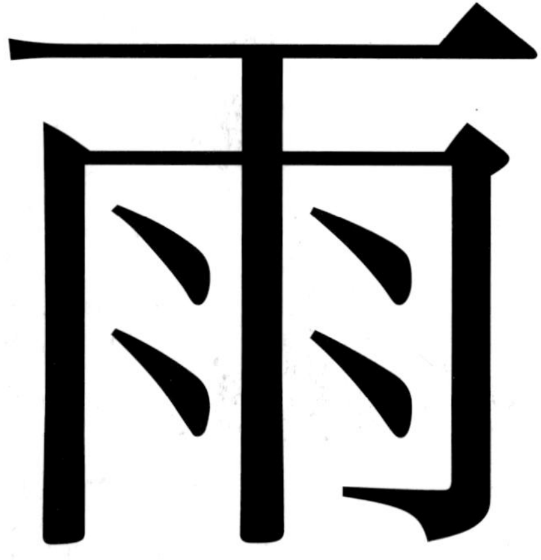

Symbol for 'rain'.

Modern Japanese writing is based on four scripts. The main one is a system of Chinese characters called *kanji*. Each character represents a different word. Some of them look a little like the word they represent. For example, the *kanji* for rain (left) includes raindrops. *Kanji* are written and read in columns from right to left. *Hiragana* characters show grammar, and the *katakana* system is used to write foreign words. Finally, *romanji* uses the English alphabet to write Japanese words, for example 'toukyou' for Tokyo.

## Words and phrases

| English | Japanese | How to say it |
|---|---|---|
| hello | konnichi wa | kon-nee-tchee wah |
| goodbye | sayonara | sah-yoh-nah-rah |
| thank you | arigato | aree-gah-toh |
| yes | hai | hi |
| no | iie | ee-eh |

**DID YOU KNOW?**
**Japanese is one of the most important languages in the world. It is spoken by about 130 million people in many countries around the world.**

**WEB LINKS**
**To find out more about Japanese, go to:**
**http://www.japan-guide.com/e/e2046.html**

## Bowing

When Japanese people meet each other they bow to show respect. The type of bow depends on the status of the person being greeted. A deep bow is for an important person. People also bow when they say they are sorry.

## Japanese sayings

The Japanese love sayings, and they use them frequently in everyday life. Here are some:

'Beautiful lotus flowers are born from mud.'

'One kind word can warm three winter months.'

'When the character of a man is not clear to you, look at his friends.'

'The reverse side also has a reverse side.'

## *Dialects*

**Different regions of Japan have different local dialects. The standard spoken dialect is the one from Tokyo. Dialects can vary across quite small areas. For example, in the Aichi prefecture in southern Honshu, the Mikawa dialect is spoken in the eastern half, while the Nagoya dialect is spoken in the western half. Other dialects include Tohoku, which is spoken in a part of northeastern Honshu, and Ibaraki, which is spoken in part of eastern Honshu.**

# Stories and Legends

*There are two main religions in Japan – Buddhism and Shintoism. Shintoism has many tales of gods and goddesses. The Kojiki, or 'Record of Ancient Things', is the oldest recognized book of the myths, legends and history of Japan.*

According to a **Shinto** myth, the world was created by the male god Izanagi and the female goddess Izanami. They stood on the floating bridge of the heavens and plunged a jewel-encrusted spear into the ocean. When they pulled it free, the water that dripped from the spear formed the first island of Japan.

## The Tale of Genji

*The Tale of Genji* (left) is a great Japanese classic. It was written by a Japanese noblewoman, Murasaki Shikibu, in the early eleventh century. The story is all about the life of Prince Genji (shown left, visiting his lover) and is full of love, betrayal and death. Some people have called this beautiful tale the world's first novel. It is also one of the earliest important works of literature written by a woman.

## Amaterasu

When Amaterasu, the Shinto sun goddess, was treated badly, she hid in a cave and the world went dark. The gods tricked her into coming out by putting a big mirror outside the cave. Then Uzume, the goddess of laughter, began to dance. Amaterasu peeped out to see what was happening and created a ray of light that is the dawn. She was so fascinated by her reflection in the mirror that she came out of the cave, and her light spread across the world. This sun is rising over the gateway to a Shinto shrine, left.

DID YOU KNOW?
**The Japanese word for emperor is *tenno*, meaning 'heavenly emperor'. The Japanese Imperial family is the oldest royal family in the world. According to Japanese mythology, the first emperor, Jimmu, was a descendant of the sun goddess Amaterasu. He was made emperor in 660 B.C.E. The Japanese believed their emperor was a god until the twentieth century.**

## Sei Shonagon

Sei Shonagon (right) was a lady at the court of the Empress Sadako during the tenth and eleventh centuries. She wrote a famous book called *The Pillow Book*, recording her observations at that time. It is thought to have been completed in 1002 C.E. In it she included many lists, thoughts about her life and the people around her, interesting events at court, and some poetry. Shonagon's creative writing and poetic skill have made this a timeless piece of literature. It is interesting to many generations of readers, as well as a valuable historical record of that period in Japanese history.

# Art and Culture

*For many centuries, Japan had little contact with the rest of the world, and the country developed a wonderful and unique culture. In the nineteenth century, when Japan opened up to outsiders, some aspects of Western culture were adopted. But for the Japanese people their traditions are still very important.*

Many of Japan's most beautiful buildings are religious temples and **shrines**. Shintoism is Japan's oldest religion, practised by ninety per cent of the population. They believe that the gods, called *kami*, live in natural places such as mountains, rivers and lakes. The gods are worshipped at shrines, where people offer a gift of food or money, and pray for health and good fortune. The entrance to a Shinto shrine is marked by a beautiful gateway called a *torii*. Visitors purify themselves here with water.

## White Heron Castle

Himeji Castle in Honshu (below) is also called White Heron Castle because it resembles a flying heron. It was expanded between 1601 and 1614 by the Tokugawa shoguns (see page 7). This magnificent castle is made of wood, and covered in white plaster to protect it from fire.

## *Paper folding*

***Origami*** **is the Japanese art of folding paper to make models. They are often animals.**

## Hokusai (1760–1849)

Katsushika Hokusai is one of Japan's most famous artists. He lived in Tokyo, which was then called Edo. His best-known works are of Japan's beautiful landscapes, especially Mount Fuji. This print by Hokusai is called *Great Wave at Kanagawa*. Mount Fuji is the snowy peak in the background.

## *Tranquil gardens*

**Japan is famous for its stylish gardens, such as the one below. Garden design is seen as an art form. Every rock, tree, bush, stream and pool is chosen and positioned carefully. The Katsura Imperial Villa, near Kyoto, was built in the Edo period and remains one of Japan's most important cultural treasures. Its gardens are a masterpiece of Japanese design, and the buildings are some of the greatest achievements of Japanese architecture. This is a window into the world of the Edo period.**

## Kabuki and Noh

There are two forms of traditional Japanese theatre – *kabuki* and *noh*. *Kabuki* is a mixture of opera, dance and music. Men, wearing elaborate costumes, act all the roles. The stories are full of love, disaster and revenge. The audience joins in with booing and hissing. *Noh* is more serious and the plays are often based on myths. Women are forbidden to take part in either form of theatre.

DID YOU KNOW?
**Flower arranging, called *ikebana*, is also a Japanese art form. Select branches are arranged according to a rigid set of rules.**

# Make Your Own Japanese Fan

*Fans were first made in Japan hundreds of years ago. You can use this pretty one to keep yourself cool on a hot day, or for decoration.*

**You will need:**

- pencil
- thick black card
- scissors
- red card
- cutting board
- craft knife
- clear glue
- 1.8 m of red thread

1 Using a pencil, draw the outline of the fan shape on a piece of black card. It should be about 20 cm across at the widest point. Cut out the fan shape.

2 Draw a handle shape on the black card. Cut it out, and then draw around it to make another handle shape. Cut out the second handle.

3 Draw the outline of another fan shape on a piece of red card, but make it 0.6 mm smaller all round than the black shape. Cut out the red fan shape.

4 Put the red fan shape on a cutting board. Then draw the outline of flowers and leaves on it. Ask an adult to help you cut out the flower and leaf outlines, using a craft knife.

5 Use a pair of scissors to cut out a crescent shape from the bottom of the red fan shape.

DID YOU KNOW?
Japanese folding fans were first invented in the sixth century. They were used by wealthy Japanese people. They were made from thin strips of wood cut from cypress trees. The strips were sewn together so that they could fold flat, or spread out to form a fan shape.

6 Glue the red fan shape on to the black fan shape, leaving the same amount of border all the way around.

7 Glue the handles on to the bottom of the fan. Glue one handle to the front of the fan. Glue another handle to the back of the fan. Put some glue down the middle of each handle, then press them together to make one handle.

8 Wind the red thread around your fingers to make lots of loops. Tie a short piece of thread around the top of these loops. Cut through the loops at the bottom to make a tassel. Tie the tassel to the handle of your fan.

# Sports and Leisure

*Japanese people are very hard-working. Workers have only one or two weeks of holiday a year. Children study hard during long terms at school, and often have extra lessons in the evening. When people do have time off, they enjoy lots of different sports and hobbies. They also like to eat out with friends and family.*

## Martial arts

**Most Japanese children learn one form of** martial art, **such as *judo*, *karate* or *kendo* (fencing, below), in school. These ancient sports developed from the fighting skills of warriors.**

Japan's national sport is **sumo** wrestling (above). It is an ancient sport where two wrestlers, called *rikishi*, attempt to force one another out of a ring. The *rikishi* lead a very disciplined life. They live in communal 'sumo training stables' called *heya*. They train hard, and eat a special diet.

DID YOU KNOW?

**More comics are sold in Japan than in any other country in the world. Japanese comic art is called *manga*. It illustrates many different subjects, including quite serious ones.**

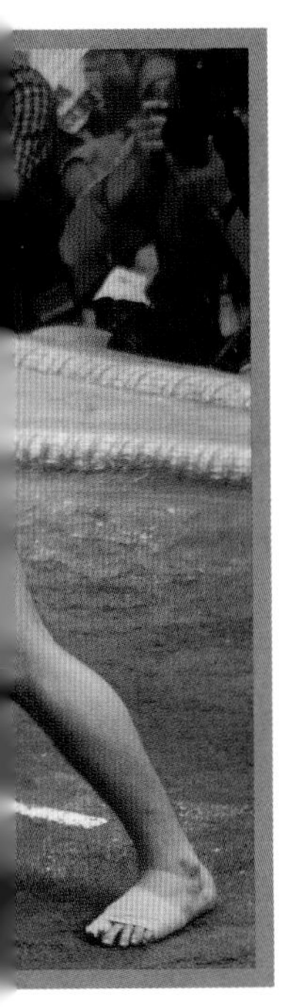

## *Bonsai*

The Japanese are particularly fond of *bonsai* – the traditional Chinese art of growing miniature trees. They are less than one metre tall, and their tiny branches are carefully wired to make beautiful shapes. They can live for over 100 years.

## *Yakyu*

**Baseball has been very popular in Japan since the nineteenth century. Today millions of Japanese people enjoy watching and playing their version of the game, which is called *yakyu*.**

## Karaoke

The Japanese love music and are not shy about performing in front of an audience. It was the Japanese who developed the idea of *karaoke* bars, where people stand up and sing along to recorded music.

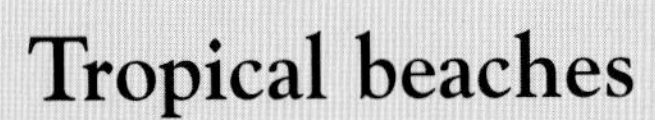

## Tropical beaches

Japan is surrounded by oceans, so there is no shortage of beaches. The sandy beaches on the islands in the Ryukyu and Bonin island chains are very popular with tourists. The sea is clear blue, and perfect for both swimming and snorkelling.

# Festivals and Holidays

*The Japanese year is filled with many religious festivals. Thirteen national holidays also take place each year.*

New Year is the biggest festival of the year in Japan. It lasts for three days and is called *Ganjitsu*. On New Year's Eve, people put pine decorations called *kadomatsu* (like the ones shown right) outside their front doors. Over the next few days people visit their families, eat special foods and play traditional games. They may also visit a Shinto shrine or a Buddhist temple, to pray for good fortune in the coming year.

WEB LINKS
Find out about local festivals at:
www.japan-guide.com/e/e2063.html

## *A Buddhist festival*

**At the Buddhist festival of Obon, in July or August, people return to their home towns to visit the graves of their ancestors. They think that their ancestors' spirits return to Earth at this time, so they light bonfires and leave food on their graves to greet them.**

DID YOU KNOW?
**Children's Day is on 5th May and celebrates children. Families all over Japan fly colourful kites in the shape of a carp (a large fish). There is usually one for each child.**

## Hanami

**In spring, Japan's cherry trees come into blossom. Japanese people celebrate the arrival of the blossom with a custom called *hanami*, which means 'flower viewing'. Families gather to have picnics and parties under the beautiful flowering branches.**

## Clothes for special occasions

A ***kimono*** is a traditional Japanese robe. It is made of fine silk, often decorated with embroidery. It is tied at the waist with a wide sash called an *obi*. *Kimonos* may be worn by both men and women on special occasions such as weddings, funerals, and graduations, and for visiting shrines.

## Sapporo Snow Festival

Every February, millions of people travel to Sapporo in Hokkaido for the Snow Festival. For seven days, the country's top ice sculptors display their work. Some of the ice sculptures can be the size of buildings several stories high. Stalls line the streets selling hot, sweet chicken and other delicious dishes. Whole lobsters are sold in blocks of ice, along with many other seafoods.

# Glossary

**abolished** banned forever
**atomic bombs** extremely powerful bombs that cause massive destruction; they use energy released when the nuclei of small particles of matter called atoms are split
**ceremonial role** representing the nation but with no real power
**characters** symbols that represent words; in Japan they are called *kanji*
**constitution** series of written rules that set out how a country should be governed
**daimyo** ruling family, or ruler
**dialects** local variations in the way a language is spoken
**dynasty** sequence of rulers from the same family
**emblem** symbol that represents something
**emperor** the male ruler of an empire
**empress** a female emperor, or the wife or widow of an emperor
**imperial** relating to the emperor, empress or empire
**inhabited** lived in or occupied by
**kimono** traditional Japanese robe with wide sleeves worn by men and women
**martial art** ancient sport, developed from the fighting skills of warriors
**monsoon** season of strong wind and rain
**nomadic** wandering from place to place
**pilgrims** people who travel on a religious journey to a holy place
**plains** areas of flat land
**prefectures** small administrative regions; Japan has forty-seven prefectures
**residential** area of a town or city in which people live; non-residential areas are where people work or shop, such as offices and shopping centres
**samurai** in the past, a member of a powerful Japanese warrior group
**Shinto** ancient Japanese religion, meaning 'way of the gods'
**shogun** in the past, the most powerful Japanese military leader
**shrines** places where gods are worshipped
**social structure** the way in which a society is organized
**sumo** traditional Japanese form of wrestling
**suspension bridge** bridge that is supported by cables that reach from tall towers to hold up the bridge crossing
**terraces** steps cut into a hillside on which crops, such as rice, can be grown; terraces are often seen in countries in Asia
**typhoons** violent tropical storms

# Find Out More

## Books

Amery, H and Cartwright, S and di Bello, P. *First Thousand Words in Japanese* Usborne Publishing
ISBN: 978 0 7460 2310 5

Bradford, Chris. *The Way of the Warrior (Young Samurai)*. Puffin
ISBN: 978 0 1413 2430 2

Lansford, L and Schwarz, C. *The Changing Face of Japan*. Wayland
ISBN 978 0 7502 4011 6

Marsh, Michael. www.franklinwatts.co.uk/GEOGRAPHY_Books_COUNTRY-FILES_Series_26389_55958.htm" \o "Country Files" Country Files: Japan
ISBN: 978 0 7496 6640 8

Sakade, F. *Japanese Children's Favorite Stories*. Tuttle Publishing, US
ISBN: 978 0 8048 3449 0

Whyte, H. *Welcome to my Country: Japan* Franklin Watts
ISBN: 978 0 7496 7021 4

Wilkes, Angela. *Internet-linked Children's World Cookbook*. Usborne Publishing
ISBN: 978 0 7460 4218 2

## Websites

**www.jnto.go.jp/eng**
This site of the Japan National Tourist Organization is arranged by themes and is easy to use.

**www.japan-101.com**
This site is packed with interesting information about Japanese places, history, culture and geography.

**www.lonelyplanet.com/worldguide/japan/**
This site is full of useful information on Japan, including its culture and places to visit.

**http://japanesefood.about.com**
This site has lots of information about Japanese food, as well as recipes for you to try.

**www.japaneseart.org**
There are wonderful examples of the best of Japanese art on this website.

# Index